Come, SING and Celebrate!

"The Night Love Was Born"   Mary Jane Mulder

"Angels We Have Heard on High Street"   J. Richard Coyle

C.S.S. Publishing Co., Inc.

Lima, Ohio

COME, SING AND CELEBRATE

8871 / ISBN 1-55673-074-8   PRINTED IN U.S.A.

Table of Contents

Table of Contents

1

The Night Love Was Born

A Christmas Program
for Children and Youth

by Mary Jane Mulder

Production Notes

Playing Time: Forty minutes.

Costumes: The toys should be dressed as their characters. Tommy and Lisa and their friends and children can be dressed in their typical Sunday clothes. The innkeepers, Mary and Joseph, and the shepherds, are dressed in robes with headcovers and bands around their heads. The angels are dressed in white robes with garland made into halos on their heads. The wisemen wear colorful robes with crowns on their heads.

Properties: Shepherds may carry staffs. Wisemen each carry an expensive-looking container as a gift. A Christmas tree with plain white lights on it is situated on the right side of the stage.

Setting: The stage is set to look like Tommy and Lisa's toy room. On the right side of the stage, toward the back, there is a large toy box, a rocking chair, and a large box for the Jack-in-the-Box. To the far right is the Christmas tree. The entrance door is at the right side of the stage. A large cross is hanging on the wall. The manger is located at center stage. Chairs for the children to sit in as they finish speaking are situated on the left side of the stage. There should be one floating microphone for the "toys" and Lisa and Tommy. Microphones are also positioned in front of the speakers who will file in as the script calls for them.

Lighting: Spotlights and full stage lighting.

Music Sources

"Wonderful Counselor"

By John Michael Talbot. Copyright 1980 by Budwing Music, Cherry Lane Music Publishing Company, Inc. From the book *Communion II*.

"Behold That Star"

Copyright 1970 by Robbins Music Corporation, New York, New York. From the book *170 Christmas Songs and Carols*.

"Come With Me"

Words and music by Anita Grund. Copyright 1967 by Heartwarming Music Company. From the book *Power To Be* by Gene, Cotton, John T. Benson Publishing Company, 136 Fourth Avenue North, Nashville, Tennessee 37219.

"Come On, Ring Those Bells"

Copyright 1976 by Manna Music Inc., 2111 Kenmore Ave., Burbank, California 91540.

Characters (in order of appearance)
    Narrator
    Raggedy Andy (doll)
    Teddy Bear (stuffed animal)
    Jack-in-the-Box (toy)
    Soldier (toy)
    Tiger (stuffed animal)
    Raggedy Ann (doll)
    Tommy (boy)
    Lisa (girl)
    14 Friends (boys and girls)
    Mary and Joseph
    Innkeepers
    Six Shepherds
    Six Angels
    Three Wisemen
    Nine Children (boys and girls)

Time: The day before Christmas in the current year.

Setting: The play room in Tommy and Lisa Graham's home. As the scene opens the toys are seated in or near the toy box. There are two dolls, one tiger, one teddy bear, a jack-in-the-box, and a soldier.

Narrator: The name of our story is "The Night Love Was Born." As the story begins, we are in the playroom of Lisa and Tommy Graham's home. The toys are relaxing around the room as they discuss the coming of Christmas. Let's listen in . . . (*Spotlight is focused on the toys sitting as though they were posed for a picture. As the first speaker begins, the toys start to move and use their hands and faces in conversation.*)

Raggedy Andy: Isn't it exciting! Only one more day until Christmas. I can hardly wait!

Teddy Bear: Tommy hugs me so tightly while he's sleeping that I can just hear his heartbeat grow faster as the day gets closer.

Jack-in-the-Box: This time of year I always wish my box would play a Christmas song for Tommy and Lisa.

Soldier: I don't know why you all get so excited about one day. What is so special about it anyway? First of all, Tommy and Lisa get all new toys and will just push us to the back of the closet. Second, I find no good reason for all of this happiness and love you think you feel at this time of the year.

Tiger: Why, Soldier, haven't you heard of Jesus? Don't you know that it is his birthday at Christmas?

Soldier: I don't know the story, but it's hard to see how one little boy's birthday could change the whole world. I'm afraid you have all grown soft from the hugging and being carried around. I have stayed in my place on the shelf and have not smiled or been cuddled. I see things more clearly than you.

Raggedy Ann: My dear Soldier, we have not grown soft. We can see the love and joy that Tommy and Lisa share with us and their friends because they love Jesus.

Soldier: I can not feel these things because I am a soldier and must stand straight and tall. I do not have time for stories about a baby being born.

Raggedy Andy: The story of Jesus is far more than just a story about a baby's birthday.

Tiger: Oh, yes! It is the story of how the Lord has given us his Son to save our lives.

Soldier: What do you mean? A baby that can save lives?

Jack-in-the-Box: Shh . . . Shh . . . Here come Tommy and Lisa now. We must be quiet. They are having some friends over tonight for a Christmas celebration. (*The toys stop all action and remain in comfortable but posed positions as Tommy and Lisa enter through the right stage door.*)

Lisa: Our friends should be here any minute, Tommy.

Tommy: I hope they remember their costumes.

(*There is a knock on the door.*)

Lisa: Oh, good, that must be them now. (*She steps to the door and opens it.*) Hi! We are so glad you could come over.

Friend 1: We were really excited when you asked us to come over and act out the Christmas story with you. It will be great fun. And what better way could there be to celebrate Jesus' birthday?

Tommy: Come on in, everyone. (*Pause while friends get through the door onto the stage. Tommy points to a friend and says:*) Why don't you start our story out?

Friend 2: The story begins long, long ago when God created the first man and woman. They did not obey God and ate of the fruit of a tree he had told them not to. Because Adam and Eve chose to disobey God, we all became sinners in God's Kingdom.

Friend 3: God loves us so much that he promised Adam and Eve that he would send a Savior to destroy Satan, who had tempted them into eating the fruit of the forbidden tree.

Friend 4: Many years later God appeared to Abraham, who was his faithful follower. He told Abraham that he would send a Savior through Abraham's line of descendants.

Friend 5: As the line of Abraham grew from Isaac to Jacob and later to David, a shepherd boy, God's promise was unfolding.

Friend 6: A prophet named Isaiah said many years before our Savior was born: "For unto us a child is born, unto us a son is given; and the government shall be upon his shoulder; and his name shall be called Wonderful, Counselor, The Almighty God, The Everlasting Father, The Prince of Peace."

Friend 7: "Of the increase of his government and peace there shall be no end, upon the throne of David, and upon his kingdom, to order it, and to establish it with judgment and with justice from henceforth even forever." That's from Isaiah 9:6-7. (*Children gather around in a semicircle as they all sing "Wonderful Counselor" or another appropriate selection.*)

Friend 8: After many years passed, this prophecy began to be fulfilled. It all started with the story of Jesus' birth. (*At this time the children who have sung move to the left side of the stage and sit as if they were expecting more friends to arrive. There is a knock at the door and Tommy goes to answer it.*)

Tommy: Oh, I'm glad to see you. You are just in time to tell us the Christmas story. Come on in. (*Friends enter.*)

Friend 9: Well, the Bible tells us that . . . In those days, there went out a decree from Ceasar Augustus, that all the world should be taxed.

Friend 10: And all went to be taxed, every one to his own city.

Friend 11: And Joseph also went up from Galilee, into Judea, unto the city of David, which was called Bethlehem . . .

Friend 12: . . . to be taxed with Mary his espoused wife, being great with child.

Friend 13: And so it was, that while they were there, the days were accomplished that she should be delivered.

Friend 14: And she brought forth her first born son, and wrapped him in swaddling clothes and laid him in a manger; there was no room at the inn.

(*Children remain standing to sing "Once in Royal David's City." After the song, the children move to the left of stage and sit waiting with the others. There is a knock at the side door and Tommy answers it.*)

Tommy: Hello. You can show us just what happened to Mary and Joseph that night.

(*Mary and Joseph and the Innkeepers enter dressed for their parts in robes and head covers. Mary and Joseph move from one innkeeper to the next as they say their lines; after each response, they move on.*)

Mary and Joseph: Knock . . . Knock . . . Knock . . .

Innkeepers (*all together*)**:** No room!

Mary and Joseph: Knock . . . Knock . . . Knock . . .

Innkeepers (*all together*)**:** No room!

Mary and Joseph: Knock . . . Knock . . . Knock . . .

Innkeepers (*all together*)**:** No room!

(*Mary and Joseph reach center stage where the manger is positioned.*)

Mary, Joseph, and Innkeepers (*turning to audience*)**:** So Baby Jesus was born in a stable and laid in a manger.

(*Mary and Joseph sit down near the manger as the Innkeepers find a place to sit at the left of the stage. There is a knock at the door and Lisa goes to the door and opens it. The children enter dressed as shepherds.*)

Shepherds (*all together*)**:** We are the shepherds who watched their flocks that holy night.

Tommy: Oh, Yes! Can you tell us what happened to you?

Shepherd 1: We saw a bright and shining light.

Shepherds (*all together*)**:** We were all afraid!

Shepherd 2: An angel came to us and said the Savior was born.

Shepherd 3: He told us not to be afraid, and that he had brought glad tidings.

Shepherd 4: The angel said a Savior was born in the city of David.

Shepherd 5: Later we found him. He was wrapped in swaddling clothes and lying in a manger.

Shepherd 6: We fell on our knees and gave thanks to God!
(*Shepherds move to stage left as there is another knock at the door. Lisa goes to the door and opens it. The angels enter.*)

Angels (*all together*)**:** We are the angels who came to sing praises to our new-born King.
(*Angels take their positions on stage to the right.*)

Angel 1: Glory to God in the highest!

Angel 2: On earth peace forever and ever . . !

Angel 3: Good will toward all men!

Angel 4: Praise His name in all of the earth!

Angel 5: Let all that is within you, praise his name!

Angel 6: He shall reign King of kings and Lord of lords!
(*Mary and Joseph, the innkeepers, the shepherds, and the angels all stand in their places to sing "Away in a Manger" and "Go Tell it on the Mountain." Angels move to the left. All children sit down on the left side of the stage. There is another knock at the door. Lisa answers it, and the wisemen enter.*)

Tommy: The three wisemen came to visit the King of kings.

Wiseman 1: I chose to bring gold to the baby who is the Savior of the world.

Wiseman 2: My gift was frankincense, to burn as an incense for this prophesied king.

Wiseman 3: I selected my most precious earthly possession for my new king. It is my myrrh.
(*Wisemen stand in semi-circle around microphones as they sing "Behold that star." Other appropriate music can be used. The Wisemen move to stage left and sit down.*)

Lisa: The Christmas story doesn't end here though. His life is an example of his love.

(*There is knock at the door. Tommy answers it and the children enter.*)

Tommy: Here are the children to tell us about Jesus' life.

Child 1: When Jesus was thirteen he proved his knowledge of the Word to the teachers in the temple.

Child 2: He selected followers called disciples to help him spread the Good News of salvation through trust in him.

Child 3: He worked miracles and was an example of love.

Child 4: He listened to everyone, no matter how great or unimportant they were.

Child 5: He taught us how to pray.

Child 6: He said, "No one will come to the Father, but by me."

Child 7: He taught us to trust and obey his words of truth.

Child 8: Finally and completely, he died for our sins on the Cross.

Child 9: He died so that we might live in eternity with him . . . free from our sins and pain if we will only trust him. (*Storytellers remain in position and sing "Come With Me." Other appropriate music may be substituted. Children remain in their places.*)

Lisa: Before you get ready to go, let's sing a few songs and light the Christmas tree, to remember that Jesus is the Light of the World.

(*The tree is lighted as Lisa makes an exaggerated motion to turn on the lights. The children all stand to sing "Come on, Ring Those Bells" and "Joy to the World". Other appropriate music could be used instead.*)

Friends, Mary and Joseph, Innkeepers, Shepherds, Angels, Wisemen, and Children: Good-bye, good-bye. Thanks for the nice time — Good-bye! (*These players all leave the stage.*)

Tommy: We'd better get to bed too. It's getting late.

Lisa: Wasn't it fun tonight, Tommy, remembering the wonderful story of Christ's birth?

(*Tommy and Lisa exit stage and turn out the lights. Christmas tree lights are left on. The spotlight is on the toys.*)

Jack-in-the-Box: Well, soldier, did you see the love and joy Tommy and Lisa and their friends shared tonight because of the love and hope they find in Jesus?

Raggedy Ann: Listen to this song I heard Lisa singing yesterday.

(*Sing: "Love Came Down at Christmas" or another appropriate song. Raggedy Ann sings a solo from her place in the large rocking chair.*)

Soldier: You're right. I can see there is much more to Christmas. Jesus' love is real!

Tiger: The night of Christ's birth was a special and holy night. It was the night love was born.

(*Spotlight focuses on the manger and the cross. At the same time all of the other lights will be turned off. All children and the congregation sing "Silent Night."*)

2

Angels We Have Heard on High Street

A Christmas Musicale and Mime
for Youth and Adults

by Dick Coyle

Introduction

"Angels We Have Heard On High Street" is a contemporization of the Gospel account of the birth of Jesus. It is intended to ask, concerning magi, angels and shepherds, "Could they be we; could we be they?"

This dramatization was written and produced to be a supplement to the cantata, "Great Christmas Choruses," and the narration takes the place of the narrative in the cantata, with the same musical background — adjusted between organist and narrator.[1] (See page 21.)

However, it may also be used with seven traditional carols; sung either by a choir, or by the audience, or by a combination of choir and audience.[2] (See page 21.)

The action originates from within the audience for the specific purpose of fortifying the concept of the timeless and contemporary message of Christmas.

The roles, as will be seen, also carry this message in a dramatic, non-verbal portrayal.

One distinct advantage is the flexibility of the production and the minimum amount of rehearsal time involved in producing a moving and gripping experience for all participating: musicians, choir, cast and audience alike.

Two items merit special emphasis: 1) The roles allow for much flexibility and selectivity, but should involve persons who are not acting, but actually are, in everyday life, what they here portray. 2) The mime must be lively with plenty of action. Each character, especially shepherds and angels, should decide how best to portray him or herself and his or her role in life.

All the action of the mime, except for the appearance of shepherds and angels, takes place while the chorus preceding instructions is being sung. The mime is all done silently, without exchange of words.

Props for the cast are itemized in the list of cast members. Other props needed are listed below. Instructions are included in the script.

Cast

Mary — sixth or seventh grade girl, fresh and innocent-looking. Mary wears a common-looking white dress, older, perhaps a bit soiled; and a blue shawl on her head.

Joseph — sixth or seventh grade boy, dressed in denim jeans and flannel shirt.

Innkeeper — a business man, large, serious, imposing-looking, dressed in a sharp business suit.

The Magi — three men, age not very important, preferably one older youth, one young adult and one aging adult:

First Wise Man — a walker, carrying a peace sign, or a CROP Walk sign. If possible it should be a person who has participated in some kind of walk, demonstration or fund-raiser with which the church has been affiliated. A "slogan" T-shirt could also be used.

Second Wise Man — rides a bicycle; casual clothing

Third Wise Man — wheels a wheelchair; casual clothing.

The Angels (*Messengers*) — mixed ages and sexes (*adults*):
  1. *Announcer* — carries a microphone
  2. *Musician* — carries a musical instrument (*trumpet*)
  3. *Educator* — academic cap and gown, carries a book
  4. *Tele-communicator* — carries a telephone
  5. *Minister* — robe, carries a Bible
  6. *Secretary* — carries a small or toy typewriter
  7. *Juror* — judge or attorney — robe or business suit, carries a gavel
  8. *Doctor* — white jacket, carries a stethoscope

The Shepherds
  1. *Farmer* — coveralls, carries a rake
  2. *Student* — carries a pencil and pad

3. *Police Officer* — in umiform, carries a nightstick
4. *Nurse* — in uniform, carries a chart and pencil
5. *Homemaker* — dressed in apron, carries a broom
6. *Waiter (Waitress)* — in uniform, carries menus
7. *Carpenter* — casual, with carpenter's apron, carries hammer and nails
8. *Custodian* — uniform or dress clothing, carries push broom (*or pushes a sweeper*)

Props

A manger — stuffed with straw over draping blanket
A life size baby doll (*to fit manger*)
Sign on pole — PEACE ON EARTH — or (*preferably*) one having to do with a CROP WALK or other project with which the congregation can identify as having been involved
Bicycle
Wheelchair
Three boxes, wrapped as contemporary Christmas gifts
One Christmas shopping bag.

The manger can be as simple or elaborate as desired, from a simple "cradle" to a full stable. It should be placed in the center of front stage or chancel, and must be on an elevation that can be seen by audience. (*Chairs, right and left may be used for Mary and Joseph, if desired; otherwise, they alternate standing and kneeling.*) The Wise Men carry the wrapped gifts.

Time

Narration is eight to ten minutes. Chorales or carols, approximately thirty minutes.
Total performance — thirty-five to forty minutes.

Music

[1]*Great Christmas Choruses* is a series of selections from the masters, compiled and edited by Roy E. Johnson and Walter Rodby, for mixed voices (SATB) with organ/piano accompaniment. It is published by Somerset Press, a division of Hope Publishing Company, copyright 1970, Carol Stream, Illinois 60187, Code No. 356. The seven choruses are: "Break Forth, O Beauteous Heavenly Light," from "Christmas Oratorio," J. S. Bach; "There Shall A Star Come Out of Jacob," from "Christus," F. Mendelssohn; "Lo, How A Rose E're Blooming," M. Praetorius; "Glory to God," from "Messiah," G. F. Handel; "Cantique de Noel (O Holy Night)," A. Adam; "The Shepherd's Farewell," from "The Childhood of Christ," H. Berlioz; and "Praise Ye the Lord of Hosts," from "Christmas Oratorio," C. Saint-Saens.

[2]Although we strongly recommend using the above because of the impact the masters give the narrative and the overall musical and dramatic blend of classic and contemporary, the following carols may instead be used:

1. "O Little Town of Bethlehem"
2. "As With Gladness Men Of Old"
3. "Thou Didst Leave Thy Throne"
4. "While Shepherds Watched Their Flocks By Night"
5. "Angels We Have Heard On High"
6. "Silent Night, Holy Night"
7. "Joy To the World"

Note to Worship Planners: If the program is inserted in worship seting, it is suggested that it be followed by a benediction and postlude.

Narration and Instructions

1. Narrator

Mary, engaged to Joseph, was found to be pregnant, expecting a child of the Holy Spirit. Joseph, a man who lived by the book, resolved to be quietly separated, but then, an angel appeared to him and said: "Joseph, son of David, do not be afraid to go on living the life you have planned. Take Mary to be your wife, for that which is conceived in her is of the Holy Spirit. She will have a baby boy, and you shall call him Jesus — *Emmanuel* — God with us."

Christmas [is coming soon]/[is here]. Will it be no more than a remembrance of the past, or will it be for us also a time to hear an angel telling us that the Holy Spirit impregnates the near and dear to us with new birth in Christ Jesus? Will it be a time for us to hear a voice that conveys courage — courage to go on living the life we have planned even though the script may not be turning out the way we wrote it? Will Christmas, 19__, simply scintillate our sentiments or will it sensitize our spirits? Is *God* with *us*?

2. First Chorus

3. Narrator

"Now when Jesus was born in Bethlehem of Judea in the days of Herod the king, behold wise men from the East came to Jerusalem, saying, 'Where is he that is born King, for we have seen his star in the East, and have come to worship him.' "

Who are the wise who follow that star and journey to seek a King and the Peaceable Kingdom? Do we not meet them along the way of our own pilgrimage? Might they be we? Might we be they? Do they not venture today, bearing gifts of unique personality, nationality, culture and skill? Do they not travel our streets and highways like those who walked from the west coast to the nation's capitol to register their heart's desire for the Kingdom to be on earth? Do they not seek a star as they ask us to sponsor them on CROP Walks and fund raisers of all sorts to bring food, hope, healing and justice to others? Are they not those who put wheels to faith, missionaries of word and healing, mobilizing commitments into actions?

Are they not they who struggle through pain, disadvantage, obstacles, handicaps and incapacities of one sort or another to seek new birth and to add their love to the love of life?

4. Second Chorus

(As the choir sings, the magi process from the rear narthex, down the center aisle and up a side aisle, returning to the narthex. This flow and all subsequent flow of the cast must be adjusted to the dimensions of the particular sanctuary in use.)

5. Narrator

Joseph and Mary arrive in Bethlehem to answer the untimely call to be counted for taxation. Bethlehem bustled and the world, as usual, hustled. Headlines told of the thousands of scheckels visitors would bring into the city. But, for Mary and Joseph there was no welcome. Big bucks often spell little room for little folks.

Jesus would say one day, "Unless *you* become as little children, there's no way you can enter the Kingdom of God." Mary and Joseph came that night like little childen — in the innocence of love, in the hope that a big and strange world had a place for them, trusting in the goodness of people who care about people. They were met with the "adult" — where life is business and management, organization and exploitation, facts and figures, and people forever demanding of children, "What will you be when you grow up?"

One man was moved with at least a little compassion. One man remembered, at least for a flash, what love is like.

One man cared to give at least a humble place, a small part, a miniscule piece of his life for God and love. And now there could be a birth of the True Human among humans.

6. Third Chorus

(Joseph and Mary walk slowly up the center aisle, apparently very tired, pausing from time to time, while Joseph embraces Mary and encourages her on. At one point, toward the front, they stretch out arms, join hands and swing around in a couple circles. They pause off to one side of manger where they are greeted by the Innkeeper — or better, if there is a door at one or other side of sanctuary, they go to it, Joseph mimes knocking and the Innkeeper opens door and greets them. Through mime and gestures, Joseph indicates journey, their plight. Innkeeper indicates no room, refusal, go away. Then he hesitates; facial expression indicates a melting of heart, wipes tear from eye, leads them to manger and indicates its availability. Mary and Joseph kneel at sides of cradle. The Babe has already been placed there, but not high enough to be visible to the audience. Mary reaches in to the manger and holds up the Babe, passing it to Joseph, who kisses it and hands it back to Mary. Throughout the remaining pageant, Mary and Joseph alternatively hold the child or place it in the manger.)

7. Narrator

It was to shepherds, working the night shift, that good news of great joy was announced: a Savior, Christ the Lord! It was to shepherds that the host of heaven sang of "Peace on earth and goodwill among humanity."

Who are shepherds? Are they not those who toil, day-in and day-out, to put food on our tables, to tend the machines of industry, to put us in touch with one another, to care for our social needs? Might they be we? Might we be they: — farmers and students, police officers and nurses, homemakers and waiters, carpenters and custodians? *(If changes are made in cast, they should also be made here and/or in reference to angels, following.)*

(At this juncture, the shepherds rise from where they have been sitting in reserved seats out along both sides of center aisle and begin miming their occupations in the center aisle.)

Who are God's messengers? Who dares still to proclaim good news in all they do and to point the world toward the Peaceable Kingdom? Might they be we? Might we be they: announcers and musicians, educators and tele-communicators, ministers and secretaries, jurors and doctors?

(At this juncture, the angels rise from where they have been sitting in reserved seats spaced out along the outside pew sections. They stand back and face toward center and shepherds, miming their occupations and occasionally with one hand making gestures of proclamation.)

8. Fourth Chorus

(Pantomime between shepherds and angels continues through this chorus. As the chorus ends, the angels return to their seats.)

9. Narrator

"And when the angels went away, the shepherds said to one another, 'Let us go over to Bethlehem and see this thing that has happened, which the Lord has made known to us.' And they went in a hurry and found Mary and Joseph, and the baby lying in a manger."

Holiday! A few hours away from the daily grind to celebrate Christmas. Shall we find Bethlehem near at hand for us? Shall we approach with expectancy and anticipation and savor the joy of being alive, human and alert to love and life and birth? Will we need to have a map drawn for us, or will we find the center of being and the manger of our re-birth by the instinct of thankful adoration?

10. Fifth Chorus

(The shepherds beckon to one another to follow. They go up center aisle. Those who carry trade implements rest them nearby, out of view of manger. Then they kneel, four to each side, leaving room at front for wise men. They raise their arms in various gestures of gratitude and adoration. Mary and Joseph show them the Babe. The magi reappear up center aisle. Each hands his gift to Joseph who shows it to the Babe and then places it in the shopping bag by cradle. Two kneel in front of cradle, one remains in wheelchair. Heads are bowed in deep reverence.)

11. Narrator

"And the shepherds returned, glorifying and praising God for all they had heard and seen as it had been told them. But Mary kept all these things, pondering them in her heart."

The holiday ends. Factory, classroom and kitchen beckon for attention. The beat goes on! Herod's "good ol' boys" are in hot pursuit of the wise men. Off in heaven, an angel with heavy heart prepares to tell Joseph he cannot go home, but must make tracks for Egypt. And the beat goes on! The world cries out for scientific discovery, just laws, new medical technology, a morality that works, peace and God. And the beat goes on! But the exit from the manger has an excitedly different aura about it. The return glorifies and praises God; and all who hear of those who have truly gathered at the manger wonder at what they are told. "Something is here that was not here before!" Oh, what joy, what profound, sad-happy joy dwells in our midst. Jesus has a family and we have a Savior. Truly, "The people who walked in darkness have seen a great light," and the people who have been to the manger, "On them has the light shined."

12. Sixth Chorus

(The Shepherds leave and take their seats, taking their implements with them.)

13. Narrator

"Lord, now let your servant depart in peace, according to your word and promise: for my eyes have seen your salvation which you have prepared in the presence of all — a light for revelation to the Gentiles, and for the glory of your people Israel."

14. Seventh Chorus

(The wise men exit up the center aisle to narthex. Joseph, carrying the shopping bag of gifts, and Mary, carrying the baby, exit through a side door.)

About the Authors

Mary Jane Mulder lives with her husband, Bruce, and her two girls, Kelly, age ten, and Lanae, age eight, in Willmar, Minnesota.

Mary Jane teaches second grade and also has a part-time job writing a humorous column for the local newspaper. Because of her love of children and her enthusiasm for writing she wanted to write a play for the children of her church to use at Christmas.

The Mulder family enjoy their summers in West Central Minnesota where there are many beautiful lakes. Recently they started cross-country skiing and are excited about sharing many more winters exploring the State Park that is not far from their home.

A graduate of United Theological Seminary, Dayton, Ohio, Rev. **J. Richard (Dick) Coyle** has served as a pastor for thirty years in the United Methodist and United Church of Christ denominations.

He is a native of Johnstown, Pennsylvania, married to the former Phyllis Ann Kraft, of that city, and father of three children.

Associate Pastor of St. John's United Church of Christ, Dover, Ohio, Dick helps develop thematic and integrated worship programs and special services. He chairs the Mission Priority Coordinating Committee and teaches care-giving ministry in the "Partners In Ministry" lay school for the Eastern Ohio Association of his denomination. He serves locally on the Boards of the Salvation Army and Hospice of Tuscawaras County.

In addition to writing, Dick enjoys calligraphy, computers fishing and photography.